THE ESL SONGBOOK

Eleanor Adamowski

TORONTO

OXFORD UNIVERSITY PRESS

1997

Oxford University Press
70 Wynford Drive, Don Mills, Ontario M3C IJ9

Oxford   New York
Athens Auckland Bangkok Bombay
Calcutta Cape Town Dar es Salaam Delhi
Florence Hong Kong Istanbul Karachi
Kuala Lumpur Madras Madrid Melbourne
Mexico City Nairobi Paris Singapore
Taipei Tokyo Toronto

and associated companies in
Berlin Ibadan

Oxford is a trademark of Oxford University Press

This book is printed on permanent (acid-free) paper.

Canadian Cataloguing in Publication Data

Adamowski, Eleanor
        The ESL songbook

ISBN 0-19-541283-4

1. English language - Textbooks for second language learners.* 2. Songs - Texts. I. Enkin, Marc. II. Enkin, Rebecca.
III. Title.

PE1128.A365 1997   428.3'4   C96-932494-4

Managing Editor: Monica Schwalbe
Editor: Maryrose O'Neill
Cover and interior design: Brett Miller
Cover and interior illustrations: Carol Biberstein
Page composition: Linda Mackey
Music page composition: Elma Miller

Printed and bound in Canada
1 2 3 4   97 98 99 00

Contents

About the Author and Songwriters

Eleanor Adamowski is a LINC program supervisor for the Toronto Board of Education. She has an M.A. in English (Linguistics) from York University and has taught ESL in a variety of settings including community programs, universities, and the Canada/China Language and Cultural Program. Her textbook *Canadian Stories: A Cultural Reader for ESL Students* (Prentice-Hall Canada) explores the cultural aspects of literature.

Marc Enkin is a composer and musician in Toronto. He manages the Village Studio, a music school and recording studio, where he writes and produces songs and records talking books.

Rebecca Enkin is a jazz-pop singer in Toronto. She has performed as part of the Toronto DuMaurier Downtown Jazz Festival and recorded *Rebecca Sings Barry J.'s Standards* for Fanfare Records.

Songs in *The ESL Songbook* were written by:

Don't Give Up	Eleanor Adamowski Rebecca Enkin
What are You Gonna Do Today?	Marc J. Enkin Rebecca Enkin Eleanor Adamowski
What Do You Do When You Feel Ill?	Eleanor Adamowski Marc J. Enkin
I Woke Up This Morning	Eleanor Adamowski Marc J. Enkin
Good-bye	Eleanor Adamowski Marc J. Enkin
Seasons Come and Go	Eleanor Adamowski Marc J. Enkin
Sing Me Your Song	Eleanor Adamowski Rebecca Enkin
If I Won a Million Dollars	Eleanor Adamowski Marc J. Enkin
It's Hard to be Polite in English	Eleanor Adamowski Marc J. Enkin
I Dreamt I Was a Child Again	Eleanor Adamowski Marc J. Enkin

Acknowledgements

I wish to thank my partners in this project: Marc Enkin of the Village Studio who first suggested that we compose music for ESL and was co-writer, arranger, musician, singer, and producer for the cassette, and Rebecca Enkin who was co-writer, singer, and consultant. They never lost their enthusiasm and made all of the work fun.

Many others have my gratitude for their invaluable suggestions, especially Kathy Simo, Judy Andersen, Trudy Kennell, and Nancy Fretter. Bruce Russell and Kay Farrell used the songs in classroom settings and gave important feedback. The instructors at the Hungarian House LINC program in Toronto kindly gave me advice and support, and Yvonne Brockman most generously shared her ideas about songs. I am also grateful for Susan Ehrlich's advice on pronunciation, but any errors are mine.

Many students have taught me the practicality of asking students to play with poetic language and given me poems I treasure. Natalie Adamowski's poetry has been my inspiration.

Special thanks to the staff at Oxford University Press, especially Robert Doyle, Monica Schwalbe and Yvonne MacMillan, to my editor Maryrose O'Neill, and to the anonymous readers for their helpful suggestions.

I would also like to say a special thank you to Jeff Peacock on guitar, and to Robyn Cross, Hayley Stolee Smith, and Derek Green from the Village Music Children's Choir for joining their voices to "Sing Me Your Song."

To the Teacher

People have been singing and listening to songs for as long as we can remember. Songs awaken the senses, ease tension, and make many kinds of learning easier. In the language classroom, students respond with pleasure to the rhythms of music and song.

The ESL Songbook includes ten original songs in various musical styles for students at the high beginner to advanced levels. The songs, composed especially for adult and secondary school students, are related to themes commonly taught in ESL classes. All songs are recorded on the accompanying cassette.

The ESL Songbook also includes a number of language activities and exercises, with a special focus on listening and pronunciation skills. The book offers the following for each song:

- an **introduction** to provide context
- **listening tasks** such as jotting down key words, cloze exercises or listening for the main idea
- a **pronunciation focus** on features such as linking and reduction
- **cultural discussion questions** to stimulate discussion and encourage cross-cultural communication
- **activities** to encourage communicative competence
- **tips on grammar** that is used in the song
- **extension activities** on poetry for more advanced students
- the **song lyrics** along with a glossary of selected words and expressions
- **transcriptions of the music** at the back of the book for student/teacher musicians

The ESL Songbook is also appropriate for independent learning and provides answers to those questions that ask for a definitive response, such as activities in the "Pronunciation Focus" sections. There are also a few suggested answers where students are asked to paraphrase a song or poem. Other activities are open-ended. Activities with a checkmark (✓) beside them in the book have answers in the Answer Key.

Using Songs for Language Skills

Listening Comprehension and Aural Memory

Songs help language learners expand their listening comprehension. The listening task can vary according to the level of the language learner. Listening activities can be made multi-level by asking different students to do different tasks while listening to the same song. Examples of listening tasks include the following.

Listening for the gist (general idea) of the song

The first time students listen to an uncomplicated song, they can often get the general idea (gist) of it, even without jotting down key words. For example, if they listen to "Don't Give Up" and get the idea that it is about how hard it is to learn English and how important it is not to give up, they have succeeded in getting the gist of the song.

Listening for specific information

In the classroom students get used to listening for times, places, directions, and instructions. In songs they listen for information that adds to the general idea and makes the song interesting. For example, in the song "Seasons Come and Go," they can listen for the description of summer— the skies are blue and clear. Students bring their knowledge of the world to this kind of task and can compare seasons in different countries.

Listening for key words

When skilful second language readers look at passages for the first time, they concentrate on key words, such as nouns and verbs, to try to understand the main idea of a passage. They skip over words they do not recognise or guess at their meaning from the context.

Similarly, skilful second language listeners do not try to catch every word in a spoken or sung passage they hear. Rather, they listen for key words such as nouns, verbs, adjectives, and adverbs since these words carry most of the meaning in a message. If students listen to a song and jot down the key words they hear, they can later put the words into an effective paraphrase. For example, "I Woke Up This Morning" begins

> I woke up this morning
> And surveyed the room.
> It was dirty and dusty
> So I grabbed a broom.
> I do not like cleaning
> That's one thing for sure
> But I can't stand the mess, even more.

Key words students might write down are

> woke, morning, room, dusty, dirty, grabbed, broom,
> not like, cleaning, can't stand, mess

Working in pairs, students can add to each other's list of words, and together they can come up with a paraphrase of the song that might look like this

> Someone woke up in the morning in his room. The room was dusty and dirty. He grabbed a broom and cleaned up. He does not like cleaning but also does not like mess.

By putting key words on the blackboard, the teacher can help beginners get used to listening for important words such as nouns and verbs, rather than listening to every word with equal attention.

Listening for attitudes

When students understand the general idea of a song as well as some specific information in it, they should be able to discern attitudes in the song. Is the singer happy, sad, optimistic, pessimistic, frustrated, laid-back, etc.? What can be said about a song's "attitude" if it describes summer, spring, and fall in only positive ways? Talking about attitudes provides a good opportunity to develop descriptive language that includes abstract concepts such as optimism. Such discussions help bring learners closer to being able to describe their own complex feelings in English.

Dictation

Songs can be dictation. Instead of listening for key words, students try to get down as many words as possible. Then with partners they can reconstruct a verse or chorus. This is an advanced-level exercise requiring an advanced knowledge of vocabulary and grammar. Even so, instructors should stop the tape after every one or two lines so as not to exhaust or frustrate students.

Note-taking, summarizing, paraphrasing

Advanced students can listen to a verse or chorus and take notes, that is, write down what seems important. Practising with writing down key words and gist helps students move to effective note-taking. After note-taking, students can work with partners either to summarize the passage (give the main idea and most important points) or to paraphrase it (tell what the song says in their own words). Paraphrases are usually similar in length to the original while summaries are shorter than the original.

Aural memory

An important part of listening comprehension is aural memory. Learning a new language is, to a large extent, a memory task. Students have to store new vocabulary, structural patterns, and sound patterns in short-term memory and be able to recall them later for use in communication with other people. Since repetition and rhyme often make songs easier to remember than conversations or prose, songs can be memorized by students to strengthen aural memory.

Clozes and strip stories

High-beginner students may need to see some of the words to a song before they perform a listening task. A cloze exercise helps beginners to focus their listening and feel successful even if they cannot understand all of the lyrics; a cloze also helps more advanced students when the lyrics are complicated.

A cloze exercise can be custom-made for a particular group of students. Input the lyrics on computer and blank out the words you want students to fill in as they listen. For example, blank out words that can be predicted by repetition and rhyme:

What are you gonna do today?
Oh, what are you _____ _____?
Sometimes I work, and sometimes I _____
Oh, what are you _____ _____ today?

You can also focus on verb tenses, descriptive adjectives, or content words.

Students enjoy manipulating lyrics into strip stories. The lyrics are cut into strips of one, two, or four lines. As they listen, either individually or in pairs, students rearrange strips of mixed-up lines into their proper order. End words that rhyme make this task easier. Students can also rearrange mixed-up words in a line of the song.

Strips also work well with lines of poetry. Rearranging lines in the correct order helps advanced students develop a better sense of coherence and cohesion.

Pronunciation

For spoken English to be comprehensible and sound natural, it needs to have English rhythm, stress, and intonation. English is a stressed-time language. The time it takes to say a sentence depends on the number of stressed syllables. Many other languages (such as Polish, French, Cantonese, and Spanish) are syllable-timed. The time required to say a sentence depends on the number of syllables the sentence contains.

For English to sound natural, modifications, such as the linking and reduction of syllables, are necessary in connected speech.[1] These modifications of sounds in connected speech are difficult for students to hear and use, especially if, in their language, they must fully sound final consonants or stress every syllable. But if students understand the reasons for contracting, reducing, and linking in English speech, they may feel more comfortable and adjust more quickly to the rhythm and intonation of English.

---

[1]For detailed explanations of rhythm, stress, and intonation, as well as consonants and vowels, see *Teaching American English Pronunciation* by Peter Avery and Susan Ehrlich, Oxford University Press, 1992.

These modifications are explained briefly in the section "To the Student"; teachers can decide how much detail is appropriate for their students. Even without understanding why they must make modifications, students will make the modifications as they become comfortable with the rhythm of songs.

Songs are especially useful for teaching rhythm and intonation because the melody of a song acts as a guide and helps with fluency and flexibility in intonation patterns. Students who do not wish to sing can internalize the rhythms by chanting.

Vocabulary, Idioms, and Grammar in Context

One of the important skills developed through reading fictional stories—using context to guess at the meaning of idiomatic words and phrases—is also developed through listening to and reading songs. Although songs can be formal expressions of poetic feeling (classical songs, especially), popular songs are often informal in language—conversational and full of the idioms of everyday speech.

Popular songs, and songs written for ESL learners (such as those in *The ESL Songbook*), show language in natural contexts that help with meaning. For example, in the song "Don't Give Up," the line "When life gets you down" is followed by "And you're wearing a frown." If students understand the meaning of the idiom "gets you down," they can easily predict the meaning of "frown," or vice versa. The music and the expression in the singer's voice can also help with idiomatic meaning, for example, the emphasis in the line in that same song: "English class is *driving me crazy!*" Teachers can give students the chance to guess at word meanings from context.

Songs also show grammatical structures in natural, idiomatic contexts. One of the most difficult structures for students to learn formally is the conditional tense in all its variations. Yet, there are many popular songs which use the real and unreal conditionals. The popular song "If I Loved You"[2] shows the unreal conditional in a delightful way, and learners can see how it works in the "real world." In *The ESL Songbook* "Sing Me Your Song," "If I Won a Million Dollars" and "It's Hard to be Polite in English" all show a conditional in context.

Exploring Cultural Attitudes

Popular songs show cultural behaviour and cultural attitudes. People sing about feelings, and feelings can sometimes be surprising to others and stimulate interesting discussions in a classroom. In *The ESL Songbook* "I Woke Up This Morning" shows customs surrounding household chores, as well as attitudes towards cleaning, cooking, and complaining about neighbours. These attitudes encourage a student response, as does the song about the variety of things you can do "when you feel ill."

---

[2]"If I Loved You" from *Oklahoma*, 1943, Richard Rodgers and Oscar Hammerstein, II. Copyright Williamson Music Inc.

Culture comes into a language-learning classroom through the language itself. For instance, colours have different connotations in different cultures, and so "blue skies" and "grey skies" and "the blues" all need a cultural explanation. Even the phrase "What are you going to do today?" implies that people have choices, that diversity is acceptable, and that planning a day's activities is not a bad thing, all of which are Western ideas that we might take for granted as being universal. Since most people in a new culture feel ethnocentric at first as a defense against change, discussion of differences can make people feel more comfortable, especially in a multicultural milieu where there are many right ways to do things. As students think about and articulate aspects of their own culture, they become cultural teachers.

Exploring Poetry and Verse

Just as school children need music, drama, and art to develop into well-rounded adults, most adult learners appreciate the opportunity to listen to music and play with language, activities that appeal to the aesthetic side of human nature. Like stories, songs give students a context in which to talk about hopes, dreams, and feelings. Like poetry, songs say things in a fresh way that gives us pleasure.

Often when advanced students get interested in songs, they begin to write verses or tell stories. Expressive language, the form used by creative writers, seems to grow when instructors introduce music (or literature) into the ESL curriculum.

The poems, verses, and playful rhymes in *The ESL Songbook* can stimulate both the imagination and creative writing. Students who are struggling with other skills in the classroom may get the chance to shine in this kind of activity. If your advanced students are open to it, let them show what they can do in the Extension Activities that follow the songs.

Practical Suggestions for Using the *Songbook*

- Review the themes and structures in *The ESL Songbook* (listed in the Contents) and choose a relevant song to illustrate topics, structures, and pronunciation points as the need arises.

- Select activities that are most appropriate for the level and needs of your students. You don't need to do all of the activities that accompany each song. You may also add to or adapt the activities in the book or create some of your own to meet the needs and interests of your students.

- The first four songs are short and easy, but students at a more advanced level can use them to improve the fine points of their pronunciation (stress, rhythm, and intonation). More advanced students can also do dictation—a task that is not easy—as they hear the song a second time. When songs are challenging, as the last songs in this text may be, students can be given a simpler task such as listening for the main idea or scanning for specific information.

- Don't worry if you cannot sing. The cassette is there to help you. Saying the words for the students in a natural way (phrase by phrase, rather than word by word) is important too.

- Don't force students to sing. Let them hum along for a while. On the other hand, don't abandon the song if they don't sing. It's important for students to listen to the rhythm.

- Give the students an opportunity to listen to a song just for enjoyment before they are given a task to perform. When they have a task, let them listen to the song more than once so they can be successful in completing the task.

- Although songs are a popular way to end the week when students and teachers need a pick-me-up, use the songs when students are fresh and ready for serious practice of skills like pronunciation as well.

- Apply to songs the pedagogical principles of introduction, practice, and review. Once students have learned a song they like, return to it often so that students experience the pleasure of knowing how to do something well in English. Many of the songs in *The ESL Songbook* have multiple-use themes; for example, "Seasons Come and Go" can be sung as often as weather changes. "I Woke Up This Morning" can be sung whenever lessons touch on work or housing (landlord/tenant relationships).

- Use the introductory illustration that opens each song to get students interested in the topic and ready to understand the main idea of the song.

- Raise the cultural discussion questions either before or after the song to get students interested in the content.

- Some students will need a grammatical or pronunciation focus to feel that songs are a legitimate use of their class time. Others will intuitively know that songs are a useful aid to language learning. For the sake of the sceptics, define the focus and stress the purpose of each lesson.

- Composing songs and verses can be a fruitful group activity for students. However, some students may need a quiet time to be creative.

- Show the musical notations to students who play instruments. They will enjoy sharing their musical talent, and everyone will enjoy the live music.

Further Reading

Avery, P. and Ehrlich, S. 1992. *Teaching American English Pronunciation*. Oxford: Oxford University Press.

Gilbert, J. B. 1984. *Clear Speech: Pronunciation and Listening Comprehension in American English*. Cambridge: Cambridge University Press.

Laroy, C. 1995. *Pronunciation*. Oxford: Oxford University Press.

Woods, H. *Contact Canada*. Ottawa: Public Service Commission of Canada. Especially *Rhythm and Unstress* (1979) and *Intonation* (1977).

To the Student

You may already be listening to songs in English for enjoyment, but have you thought of how songs can help improve your listening and pronunciation skills?

Each language has a "music" of its own. Have you ever said something with perfect English grammar and found that your listener did not understand you? Perhaps the "music" was not quite right. Some languages, such as Japanese and French, have a regular steady beat—TA TA TA TA. English is more irregular and has a combination of loud and soft sounds in each sentence—ti TA ti ti TA ti.

The rhythm patterns of languages with a steady beat look like this:

The rhythm of a *syllable-timed* language[*]

Syllable-timed languages put stress on each syllable (either major or minor stress). The time it takes to say a sentence depends on the number of syllables.

English is a stress-timed language. Some syllables are stressed (said louder, longer, higher). Other syllables are unstressed (short, unclear). The irregular patterns of English look like this:

The rhythm of a *stress-timed* language[*]

---

[*]From *Teaching American English Pronunciation* by Peter Avery and Susan Ehrlich (Oxford: Oxford University Press, 1992). Reprinted by permission of Oxford University Press.

The time it takes to say an English sentence depends on the number of syllables that are stressed.

Stressed syllables are generally in words that carry the meaning in a sentence: content words such as nouns, main verbs, adverbs, adjectives, question words, and demonstrative pronouns. Other words such as articles, prepositions, auxiliaries (for example, *will*, *have*, forms of the verb "*to be*"), pronouns, conjunctions, and relative pronouns, are usually *unstressed*. In the sentence, "I will come home on the train," the content words are "come," "home," and "train," and those are the words that get stressed.

Because only content words get stressed, it should take the same amount of time to say

"I will cóme hóme on the tráin."

as it does to say

"I cáme hóme láte."

The first sentence has seven syllables, and the second sentence has four syllables, but both sentences have only three *stressed* syllables. To say the first sentence in approximately the same amount of time as the second sentence, we have to "contract," "reduce," and "link" words.

- We contract words by joining an auxiliary verb to a pronoun, dropping the first consonant and a vowel: "I will" becomes "I'll."

- We reduce words by shortening unstressed words or syllables: "the train" becomes "th' train."

- We link words by blending words together: "home on the train." These words are linked because a word beginning with a vowel sound (on) comes after a word ending in a consonant sound (home). The two words sound like one word (homon). This blending happens often in English. Other examples of linking are

"Don't give up": "givup"
"I want to sing": "wanto"

When English is spoken without contracting, reducing, and linking, it sounds choppy and difficult to understand. With these modifications, the rhythm of English is maintained.

The songs in *The ESL Songbook* will also help you to practise English rhythms by grouping words that go together and pausing in the right places. Listen to the songs. If you sing or hum along, the rhythms of English will become easier to understand and to imitate.

While you are working with the songs, you will have the opportunity to talk about your own culture, as well as Canadian culture, through "Cultural Discussion" questions. You can sharpen your knowledge of grammar through "Grammar Tips." And if your English is more advanced, you can explore poetry through the "Extension Activities." Songs can make your language learning easier.

Don't Give Up

Theme: Learning a New Language
Pronunciation Focus: Linking
Structure: Imperative

Learning a new language can be exciting and satisfying. It can also be difficult and frustrating.

In every language learner's life there are "bad days," days when learning a new language just seems too difficult, days when we feel like giving up. When these days come, what do you do? How do you get the energy to keep going?

1

Listening to the Song

1. Listen to the song just for fun, before you look at the lyrics (the words of a song). Get in a good mood; dance, if you wish.

2. a) Listen to the song again, and write down the key words that you hear. Key words may be nouns, verbs, adjectives or adverbs.
    b) Work with a partner and use your key words to paraphrase the song—that is, tell what the song says in your own words.

3. Turn to the lyrics (pages 6–7) to check your answers.

✓ Pronunciation Focus

1. In order for sentences in spoken English to sound smooth, words in phrases often link together and sound like one word, for example, "give_up."

    The consonant sound at the end of the word "give" joins the vowel sound at the beginning of the word "up." Try saying "give" and "up" *without* linking them. Does it take a long time? Say it faster; "give" and "up" will blend together. If you want to read more about linking, you can review the notes in "To the Student" (page xiv).

    Now listen to "Don't Give Up" again and then look at the first six lines of the lyrics. Find other words that are normally linked in pronunciation. Practise saying the linked words in phrases.

2. In spoken English, we often use "contractions." A contraction links two words by leaving out one or more letters. In written English, we replace the lost letter with an apostrophe. "Don't" is a contraction of "do" and "not." "It is" becomes "it's." "They are" becomes "they're." "Were not" becomes "weren't."

    Name three other contractions in the song and put them into new sentences. Say the sentences with the contractions until the shortened form sounds "right."

3. Listen to the song again and then sing the song. Do you notice how the music forces you to move from word to word quickly and to link words together?

Cultural Discussion

1. "Don't Give Up" is advice and encouragement for language learners who are discouraged. Is learning English difficult for you? What parts of the language are difficult? What parts are easier? Compare your answers with the answers of other students in your class.

2. Do you have any expressions in your first language that mean the same thing as "Don't give up"? Try to translate one of these expressions into English and explain what it means.

3. When you are feeling frustrated, what do you do to make yourself feel better? What makes you keep on trying?

4. When you are feeling discouraged, do you like to be "cheered up" or would you rather be left alone?

Activities

1. What advice would you give to someone who is just beginning to learn English? Make a list of suggestions you would give to ESL students. Compare your list with a partner's. Then ask another partner and make a report of all three lists of suggestions.

2. Make a list of some of the other difficult subjects or skills that you have learned. You can include any action that you found very hard when you first tried to do it. How did you learn that subject or skill?

3. Look at the illustration of the students on page 1. What do you think each is thinking? Which one will find language learning easier? Why? Find out how many people in your class agree with you.

Grammar Tip

We use imperatives to tell people what to do, to advise them and to encourage them. Note how the imperative (command) form of a verb can be used for giving friendly advice: "Don't give up."

✓ **Extension Activities**

1. Popular songs are usually about people's feelings. Some songs are happy; some are sad. "Don't Give Up" tries to cheer up a person who is feeling discouraged. Songwriters often write about "the blues," feelings we get when we're lonely or sad. Hearing sad songs puts us in touch with our own sad feelings, and, perhaps not surprisingly, we like such songs. The country-western singer and songwriter, K. T. Oslin, begins the chorus of a song with these memorable lines about feeling "low," which is another way of saying "feeling sad."

    > Tell me, where is a woman to go
    > When she's feeling low
    > And all she wants to do is feel a little better?
    >
    > *K.T. Oslin and Gerry Gillespie, "Where is a Woman to Go?"*

    K.T. Oslin's remedy for feeling low is to listen to music that makes her cry. Why do you think people listen to sad music when they are feeling low? Is this a good remedy for you? Why or why not?

2. Songs such as "Where is a Woman to Go?" sound like ordinary conversation, but they express feelings in a fresh way that makes them interesting. Such songs are like poems set to music. However, *poems* do not have to follow the same rules as ordinary conversation. Poets play with words in creative ways to express their feelings.

    Look at how nineteenth-century American poet Emily Dickinson described "hope" in this excerpt from a poem:

    > "Hope" is the thing with feathers—
    > That perches in the soul—
    > And sings the tune without the words—
    > And never stops—at all—
    >
    > *Emily Dickinson, "'Hope' is the thing with feathers"*

    Explain Emily Dickinson's description of hope in your own words.

3. Notice how "hope" is compared to something with feathers. When writers express similarities between unlike things, such as comparing hope to a bird, we call the comparison a metaphor. If a comparison uses the words "like" or "as," it is called a simile. If the poet had said "Hope is *like* the

thing with feathers," that would be a simile. Similes and metaphors make descriptions new and fresh, for example:

> Loneliness is a sickness
> that's deep inside your soul
> that is crying to be full...
>
> *Natasha, "Loneliness"*

Why is loneliness compared to a sickness? What does "crying to be full" mean? How would you describe loneliness, or happiness, or homesickness in a new way, *your* way?

DON'T GIVE UP

Introduction

1   There are days when I wish
2   I had stayed in bed.
3   The whole world seems cold and hazy.
4   My teachers are nice
5   But they don't understand
6   *English class is driving me crazy!*

Chorus

7   Don't give up!
8   Don't give up!
9   When you think all is lost,
10   Don't give up!

Verse 1

11   When life gets you down
12   And you're wearing a frown,
13   Look up and around.
14   Don't give up!
15   There's a nip in the air,
16   And you're sure life's unfair,
17   But you must not despair.
18   Don't give up!

(Repeat Chorus)

(Musical interlude)

Verse 2

19 When life gets you down

20 And you're wearing a frown,

21 Look up and around.

22 Don't give up!

23 There's a nip in the air,

24 And you're sure life's unfair,

25 But you must not despair.

26 Don't give up!

27 Don't give up!

Glossary

to give up: to stop trying

hazy: not clear, foggy

driving me crazy: making me frustrated

gets you down: discourages you

nip: coldness

Song 2

What Are You Gonna Do Today?

Do you usually plan your day or just take things as they come? Imagine it is morning; what are all the things you can possibly do today? What are the things you have to do to take care of yourself or your family?

Listening to the Song

1. The first time you listen, just enjoy the music. Don't look at the lyrics yet.

2. The second time you listen, decide whether the day is a school day, a work day, or a "day off."

3. The third time you listen, do *one* of the following activities:
   a) Make a list of the key words (such as nouns and verbs) in the song. What does the singer say she will do? Then check your answers with a partner before you look at the lyrics.
   b) Do the following exercise. Listen to the song and fill in the blanks with the missing verbs.

What Are You Gonna Do Today?

Chorus

1 What are you gonna do today?
2 Oh, what are you _____ do?
3 Sometimes I work, and sometimes I _____
4 Oh, what are you _____ do today?

Verse 1

5 I'll _____ _____ and have a coffee,
6 Then _____ some scrambled eggs.
7 And when I'm _____ eating
8 I'll get up and _____ my legs.

(Repeat Chorus)

Verse 2

9   I'll _____ some grocery shopping
10 (The fridge at home is bare).
11 And then I'll go and _____ some clothes;
12 I haven't a thing to wear.

(Repeat Chorus)

Verse 3

13 Tonight I may _____ dancing

14 Or _____ a movie instead.

15 Then I might _____ television

16 Before I _____ to bed.

(Repeat Chorus twice)

✓ Pronunciation Focus

1. When we stress a word or a syllable in English, we say it louder and higher than other words or syllables. Certain syllables in phrases are almost always *unstressed* and reduced in order to keep to the rhythm of spoken English. For example, "going to do" is reduced to "goin' t' do" or "gonna do" as in "What Are You Gonna Do Today?" Examples of other phrases that get reduced in spoken English are:

    want to = wanna
    cup of = cuppa
    have to = hafta
    did you = didja

    You may not yet feel comfortable saying "gonna" and "wanna," but it is important to understand reduced phrases when you hear them. Reductions are for speaking. In *written* English, "gonna" is incorrect.

2. Look at these phrases: "wheredja" and "whydja."
    a) Put them into a spoken sentence.
    b) Write the full words of these phrases in a written sentence.

3. Listen to the song again. Do you notice that there is not enough time to say "What are you *going to* do today?" in the first line?

    If you want to read more about reduction, you can review the notes in "To the Student" (page xiv).

Cultural Discussion

1. For most people in North America, setting certain times to do certain things is very important. In other societies, people do not pay as much attention to schedules. Instead, they do several things at one time and don't worry about strict schedules. Do you usually make a schedule for each day? Explain your answer to a partner.

2. Do people do things like eating and shopping differently in different countries? For example, what did you eat for breakfast in the country you came from? Where did you shop for your food? Give some examples to a partner and make a list of the similarities and differences.

3. What do you do to relax? Do you like to do active things, like dancing? Do you like to do quiet things, like watching movies or television?

Activities

1. Plan an imaginary perfect day for yourself. Write a list of the things you would do. Then compare your day to another student's day. What are the similarities and differences?

2. Change the words to the first verse of the song to fit your daily routine. Then sing or say your song:

      I'll wake up and_____,

      Then _____, etc.

> **Grammar Tip**
> The verbs "going to" and "will" both express the future. The "going to" form often expresses intentions or plans, as in "I am going to go shopping today." The "will" form is often used to add details about the intentions or plans. For example, the response to "What are you going to do today?" in this song is "I'll (I will) wake up and have a coffee."

✓ Extension Activities

1. Songs like "What Are You Gonna Do Today?" are easier to remember than conversations because the message is simple. Words in the chorus are repeated, and words at the end of lines rhyme (for example, "today" and "play," "eggs" and "legs"). Rhyming words help us remember. For example, children learn nursery rhymes quickly. Have you heard the following rhyme?

      Jack and Jill went up the hill

      To fetch a pail of water   *fetch:* to go and bring back something

      Jack fell down and broke his crown   *crown:* the top part of the head

      And Jill came tumbling after.

The accented syllables are stressed (said louder and higher and longer), and the unaccented ones are unstressed. Saying this kind of rhyme is a good way to practise the rhythm of English intonation because in English the voice goes up and down more than in some other languages. Practise saying the Jack and Jill verse, paying special attention to the stress.

With a partner, make up a children's song that has the same regular rhythm. You might start like this:

> Hóng and Lí sat únder a trée
>
> And wátched the chíldren pláying....

2. Another light-hearted, adult kind of verse is the *limerick*. Limericks are five-line poems with a special rhyming scheme. The first, second and fifth lines rhyme, as do the third and fourth lines. Particular words are stressed to create a special rhythm. Read this limerick aloud with the proper stress:

    1   I knów a young ÉSL teácher
    2   Who's márried a dífficult preácher
    3   She wánts to be goód
    4   And dó what she shoúld
    5   But the preácher refúses to teách 'er.

Challenge: work with a partner to complete the first line of this couplet (two-line verse) with the same rhythm as the limerick above:

I know a young _____ _____
Who's wise and clever and prudent.

WHAT ARE YOU GONNA DO TODAY?

Chorus

1   What are you gonna do today?

2   Oh, what are you gonna do?

3   Sometimes I work, and sometimes I play.

4   Oh, what are you gonna do today?

Verse 1

5   I'll wake up and have a coffee,

6   Then make some scrambled eggs.

7   And when I'm finished eating

8   I'll get up and stretch my legs.

(Repeat Chorus)

Verse 2

9   I'll do some grocery shopping

10   (The fridge at home is bare).

11   And then I'll go and buy some clothes;

12   I haven't a thing to wear.

(Repeat Chorus)

Verse 3

13   Tonight I may go dancing

14   Or see a movie instead.

15   Then I might watch television

16   Before I go to bed.

(Repeat Chorus twice)

Glossary
gonna do: going to do
stretch my legs: stand up, after sitting down for a long time
fridge: refrigerator
bare: empty
I haven't a thing to wear: I am tired of my clothes; I want something new

Song 3

What Do You Do When You Feel Ill?

Most of us feel ill at one time or another, but we all react differently to being sick. We also use different remedies to make us feel better again. What do you do when you are sick? Do you talk about your illness, or do you keep it to yourself? Are you grumpy or cheerful? Do you have home remedies such as a special tea that makes you feel better?

Here is a light-hearted song about feeling ill and about some of the remedies for illness.

15

Listening to the Song

1. Listen once, just to enjoy the rhythm of the song.

2. Now, listen again and try to picture the actions of the two people who tell what they do when they feel ill.

3. The third time you listen, list the things that people do when they are sick to try to feel better. (Don't try to write every word; concentrate on *key words* such as nouns and verbs.) Then turn to the lyrics (pages 20–21) to check your answers.

Pronunciation Focus

1. The song, "What Do You Do When You Feel Ill?" has a special rhythm called "rap." Almost every word has one syllable and almost every syllable is stressed. This is unusual for English. The chanted words sound like a drum beating.

    Chant this song, paying special attention to the rhythm. You may have to force yourself to go faster than you wish in order to keep up with the singer. Don't worry if some words or syllables are skipped when you sing ("What d'ya do," for example). Imitating various rhythms will help you to imitate spoken English more easily.

2. Now use this rap rhythm to chant the song made up by the students in Activities #1 on the next page.

Cultural Discussion

1. What do you do to make yourself feel better when you are sick? Is this the same thing your family did when you were young?

2. In different countries, people use different remedies (cures) to get better when they are sick. Draw up a list of several remedies used in the country where you grew up. What are they used for?

    Compare your answers with those of other students. Make a new list of remedies which seem to be universal, that is, used by people all over the world.

3. Some people hide their pain. Others complain about it. Which way is better, in your opinion? Have you observed people in Canada being grumpy or cheerful when they are sick?

Activities

1. Work together in groups, listing all of your remedies for illness. Then choose four or eight of the remedies and write a verse of four or eight lines about how you would use these remedies.

    The following lines are what one group of students wrote after brainstorming.

1	When I get sick
2	I feel so bad
3	I dream so fast
4	It makes me sad.
5	I play guitar
6	I sing a song
7	I dance along
8	I feel so strong.

    Students from Hungarian House LINC Program,
    Toronto Board of Education

    Notice that the second and fourth lines of this song end with rhymed words, also the sixth and eighth lines. Rhyming words usually have endings that sound the same, for example, "ill" and "pill". However, rhyming words can have different spellings, for example, "better" and "sweater." Get in practice for writing your verse by finding all the words you can think of that rhyme with "me" and "ill."

me	*ill*
tea	pill

    Now see if you can make some of the lines in your verse rhyme.

2. Rhyming makes songs easier to remember, and rhyming can make English vocabulary easier to remember, as well. Try this experiment:
    a) First make a list of all the words you can think of that rhyme with "do" and with "pie." Remember that the endings of the words do not have to be spelled the same.

do	*pie*
blue	lie
you	sky

Then cover up your lists and write down as many of the words as you can remember.

b) Now make a list of an equal number of non-rhyming words. Then see how many words you can remember from this second list.

Which list of words were you able to remember better: The rhyming list or the non-rhyming list?

Grammar Tip

This song uses the verb "do" both as an auxiliary (helping verb) and to express an action. In the question "What do you do when you feel ill?" the first use of "do" is as an auxiliary and the second use is as a verb expressing an action.

✓ **Extension Activities**

I. The following playful verse offers some remedies for "the blues" (sadness or depression). The verse can be sung to the tune of "What Do You Do When You Feel Ill?"

> What do you do
> When you feel blue?
> Run away, or
> Throw a shoe?
>
> Sit down calmly
> And meditate?
> Or go to your room
> And vegetate?
>
> What do you do?

meditate: think quietly and deeply about something spiritual
vegetate: avoid thinking or doing anything, to become like a vegetable

Now see if you can complete this verse and make your own "poem."

What do you do
When you feel _____

_____

_____

2. Some people have very good health. Others are not so lucky. Here is a poem by Langston Hughes, the American poet, that says some people get a little bit of joy in life; some get love; and others get heaven. Good things are not given out equally.

> **Luck**
> Sometimes a crumb falls
> From the tables of joy,
> Sometimes a bone
> Is flung.
>
> To some people
> Love is given,
> To others
> Only heaven.
>
> *Langston Hughes*

> *crumb:* a very small piece of food
> *flung:* thrown away suddenly or violently

Which is the best gift, according to the poem? What words in the poem tell the answer to this question?

What would make you feel luckiest: good health, a bit of joy, or love?

What Do You Do When You Feel Ill?

Verse 1

1 What do you do when you feel ill?

2 Drink mint tea? Take a pill?

3 Go to bed for twenty-four hours?

4 Or wait for friends to bring you flowers?

Chorus

5 Some people say "I'm hurt."

6 Others hide their pain.

7 Some go a little crazy.

8 Others act quite sane.

9 Some get well fast.

10 Some get well slow.

11 How do you act when you're sick?

12 Does it show?

Verse 2

13 When I get sick, I go to bed,

14 Close my eyes, and prop my head.

15 I take a nap for an hour or two.

16 Soon I'm back to work, feeling good as new. What do you do?

Verse 3

17 When I get sick, I hate the world.

18 My hair is straight, but it gets all curled.

19   I feel like heck, and I look no better.

20   I get hot, then cold, but can't find

a sweater.

(Repeat Chorus)

Glossary

mint tea: a hot drink made
from water and mint leaves

crazy: not rational or able
to think clearly

sane: rational, reasonable

prop: put something under
something, for example,
putting a pillow under your head

nap: a short sleep

good as new: as if I'd never been sick

curled: opposite of straight

heck: (slang) "not good"–a more
polite version of "hell"

Theme: Greetings
Pronunciation Focus: Intonation
Structure: Direct Address

Good-bye

As small children, we learn to greet people when we meet them and when we leave them. In English, we say "hello" and "good-bye." In French, you would say "adieu" when you leave a friend. In Spanish, you would say "adios," and in Japanese, "sayonara." Every language has its greetings. They make everyday life more pleasant.

This song is about saying "Good-bye." It was written to tell someone leaving an English program, "Good-bye, my friend; don't forget me."

22

Listening to the Song

1. First just listen for the mood of the song. Is it happy or sad?

2. Then listen to the song as if it were a dictation. Write down all the important words you hear (nouns, adjectives, verbs), and then try to paraphrase the song (say what it means in your own words). Working on the paraphrase with a partner will make the task easier.

3. Then turn to the lyrics (page 26) and check your answers to see how many of the words of the song you caught. Compare your paraphrase of the song with those of other students.

Pronunciation Focus

1. The words, "my friend," in the line "Good-bye, my friend, farewell" are an example of *direct address*. When we use direct address in spoken English, we pause at the commas and use a lower pitch (pitch is the highness or low-ness of a sound) for the words between the commas.

    Practise saying these phrases with the proper intonation:

    > Welcome, *ladies and gentlemen*, to our class.
    > First of all, *boys and girls*, I would like to say "welcome."
    > Finally, *my friends*, I would like to say "good luck."

    Correct intonation helps your listener to understand you. For example, if we don't change pitch after the word "welcome" in the first example, a listener will think we are making a command. If we say "welcome ladies and gentlemen," it sounds as if we are telling our listener that he or she must welcome the ladies and the gentlemen.

Cultural Discussion

1. How do you say "good-bye" in your first language? Tell *all* the ways, if there are more than one. Can you translate these expressions into English? For example, in English we say "Good-bye." Once this expression meant "God be with you." We also say "See you later." This means we want to see the other person again.

    Ask other students how they say good-bye. For example, the Hebrew word for good-bye is "Shalom" which means "peace." The French word, "adieu," and the Spanish word, "adios," both mean "to God."

2. What are the gestures for "good-bye" in all the countries of all the students in your class? For example, in Canada we usually wave or shake hands.

Activities

1. Teach your instructor and all of the other students how to say the greetings in your first language. Be patient. Give individual help, if necessary. Then sing "Good-bye" again, substituting new words for the good-byes in the song.

2. Imagine that you are leaving your school and want to write a farewell speech to your fellow students. Use "direct address." Say the speech to your class.

3. What is the mood of the song, "Good-bye"? Imagine how the singer feels about saying good-bye. Describe this mood using examples from the song.

> **Grammar Tip**
> This song shows an example of direct address, as in the statement "Good-bye, my friend." "My friend" is called a vocative. Vocatives can include names or titles. We use a comma before and after a vocative in direct address: "Welcome, Mary, to our class."

✓ Extension Activities

1. "Good-bye" is a song about friendship. School children often write short verses in each other's autograph books or school yearbooks at the end of the school year. They do this to wish each other well, or to make a friendly joke. Edith Fowke has collected autograph verses about friendship and good wishes in *Folklore of Canada:*

   A friend is one who knows all about you
   And loves you just the same.

   I wish you health, I wish you wealth,
   I wish you joy in store,
   I wish you heaven after death,
   What could I wish you more?

Now make up your own verses for others in your class. You can follow one of the above formats, if you wish:

A friend is one who_____
And_____

or

I wish you_____
I wish you_____
I wish you_____

_____

Perhaps your saying can be a nonsense rhyme, for example,

Whenever I'm blue, I'll think about you, *or*
When you feel sad, pretend you're glad.

If you do this activity at the end of a course, each student can put his or her verse on a good-bye card for another student to make a memorable souvenir of the time spent together.*

2. The Chinese poet Wang Bo in the seventh century wrote this couplet on friendship:

If you've a friend who knows your heart,
Distance can't keep you apart.

a) Paraphrase this couplet. Do you agree with the feeling behind the poem? What is the poet saying here? What do you think "knows your heart" means?
b) What is a true friend? Make a list of what a friend should do for you. Compare your list to that of other students.

_____

*Suggested by Yvonne Brockman.

Song 4

GOOD-BYE

Verse 1

1   Good-bye, my friend, farewell.
2   Good-bye, my friend, adieu.
3   You will be missed, I know.
4   I hope you'll miss me too.

Chorus

5   Bye-bye, don't cry.
6   We'll be together again.
7   Bye-bye, don't cry.
8   We'll be together again.

Verse 2

9   Good-bye, my friend, adios.
10   I am sad but it won't show.
11   We've had our share of good times,
12   And now it's time to go.

(Repeat Chorus)

Verse 3

13   Good-bye, my friend, sayonara.
14   These are my wishes for you:
15   May your future be bright
16   And your troubles be few.

(Repeat Chorus twice)

Glossary
missed: thought about often
bye-bye: a short form of "good-bye"

I Woke Up This Morning

Themes: Work/Daily Routines/
Landlord and Tenant Roles
Pronunciation Focus: Grouping Words/
Reduction
Structure: Conjunctions

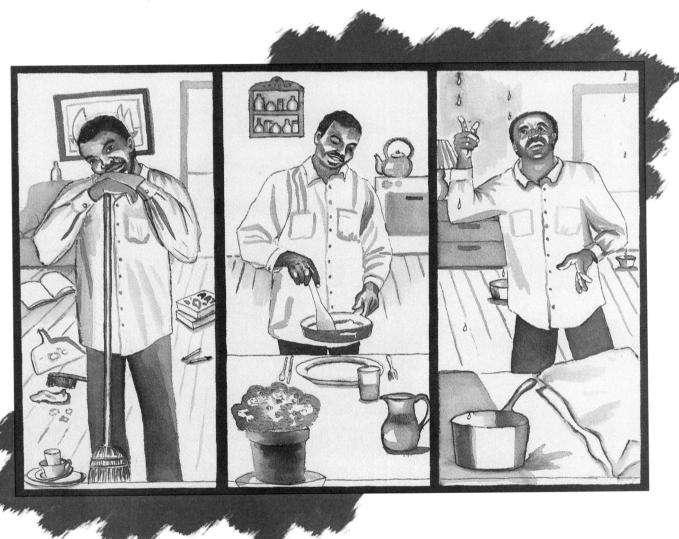

Do you like to do housework? Would you rather cook? Do you do your own cleaning and cooking? If not, who does it? Are you good at making repairs around your house or apartment?

The singer of this song has strong opinions about cleaning, cooking and making repairs.

Listening to the Song

1. This is a song in four parts. Listen to each part, first for enjoyment. As you listen, see if you agree with the singer. For example, do you like to clean? Do you like to cook?

   If you do not understand many of the words, look in the Glossary (page 38) before you listen again.

2. The second time you listen, do *one* of the following activities.
   a) Fill in the missing words in the following cloze exercise. Use the words at the top of each section.

   ### I Woke Up This Morning

   #### Part 1 (Verse and Chorus).

   dirty   room   sure   mess   cleaning   fun   bore

   1 I woke up this morning
   2 And surveyed the _____ .
   3 It was dusty and _____
   4 So I grabbed a broom.
   5 I do not like _____
   6 That's one thing for sure
   7 But I can't stand the _____ , even more.

   8 I don't like it,
   9 You don't like it.
   10 Cleaning's never _____ ,
   11 Cleaning's never done,
   12 Cleaning's never fun.

   13 I don't like it,
   14 You don't like it.
   15 Cleaning is a _____ ,
   16 Cleaning is a chore,
   17 That's for _____ .

   #### Part 2 (Verse and Chorus).

   food   cookin'   enjoy   charge   way   smile   always

   18 I woke up this morning
   19 Said, "I'm in the mood.
   20 I think I'll start _____ ,

21 I'll fix us some _____ ."

22 I do enjoy cooking

23 If I am in _____ .

24 I do it my _____ and make my portions large.

25 I enjoy it,

26 You _____ it.

27 Cookin's always fun,

28 Even just for one

29 Cookin's _____ fun.

30 I enjoy it,

31 You enjoy it.

32 Cooking makes me _____ .

33 I'm happy for a while

34 When I cook.

Part 3 (Verse and Chorus)

rain   roof   woke up   landlord   thunder   glad   tenant   fixin'

35 I _____ _____ this morning

36 And surveyed my place.

37 The _____ , it was leaking,

38 There was _____ on my face.

39 It started to _____

40 I trembled with fear.

41 Then I called the _____

42 "Please come over here."

43 "I can't do it.

44 You must do it.

45 _____ roofs is hard

46 Please be on your guard,

47 Fixin' roofs is hard.

48 You're the landlord

49 I'm the _____ .

50 What else can I say?

51 (Sometimes I am _____

52 That I rent.)"

Part 4 (Verse and Chorus)

cosy   neighbour's   morning   tidy   double   pollution   town   fun

53   I woke up this _____
54   The whole place looked fine.
55   It was _____ and _____
56   For the very first time.
57   I got out my fiddle
58   And started to play.
59   My _____ complaining
60   That I've ruined his day.

61   I'm in trouble
62   _____ trouble
63   Have to quiet down,
64   Either that, or just leave _____ ,
65   Have to quiet down.

66   Here's my solution
67   To my noise _____ .
68   "Come up and join the _____ ,
69   Two's more fun than one
70   That's for sure!"

71   Two's more fun than one
72   That's for sure!

b) Write down the key words you hear and, with a partner, use them to answer these comprehension questions. Check your answers by looking at the lyrics to the song (pages 35–38).

Part 1 (Verse and Chorus)
    1. Describe the room in Part 1 in your own words.
    2. Does the singer like to clean? How do you know?
    3. What words does the singer use to describe cleaning?

Part 2 (Verse and Chorus)
    1. What is the singer in the mood for?
    2. When and why does he like to cook?

Part 3 (Verse and Chorus)

    1. What happens to the roof?

    2. Whom does the singer call to fix the roof?

Part 4 (Verse and Chorus)

    1. What does the room look like now?

    2. How does the singer celebrate? What happens then?

    3. What's the solution to the singer's "trouble"?

✓ Pronunciation Focus

1. The rhythm of English requires words to be grouped. Pauses (breaths) come only in specific places, for instance, between phrases and clauses. For example,

    > I woke up this morning / (pause) And surveyed the room

    We generally pause at the end of a line of a song. Say each line of this song aloud with your teacher. "Chunk" the words and pause only at the end of each line.

2. Sometimes in informal spoken English, the "g" is dropped from the "ing" in words like "cooking" and "fixing." The "ing" syllables are unstressed; that is why they get shortened, or *reduced*. Find other words in this song that might lose a "g" in informal speech. For more information about reduction, see "To the Student" page xiv.

Cultural Discussion

1. Whose job was it to clean your home when you were a child? Is it different now? What did you do, as a child, to help around your home? Why do some people enjoy/hate cleaning?

2. Whose job was it to cook the food when you were a child? Is it the same now? Why do some people enjoy/hate cooking?

3. In your city, which repairs are a landlord's responsibility and which are the tenant's responsibility? Would this answer be different in other countries?

Activities

1. Write a dialogue with a partner of a scene where the landlord refuses to fix the roof. The tenant should be assertive (confident of his/her rights

but nevertheless polite) but not aggressive (angry or threatening). Ask the class to decide whether your tenant is assertive.

2. Give an example of a neighbour being "too noisy." Compare your example with another student's. Does everyone in the class agree on what "too noisy" means? What do you say to a neighbour who is too noisy? What do you say if you are accused of being too noisy? Is this the same in all countries?

3. Work in groups to practise the past tense and improve your memory with a "chain" game that begins with the title of this song, "I woke up this morning." The first student says, "I woke up this morning" and adds a fact such as "and brushed my teeth." The next student says, "I woke up this morning and brushed my teeth," and then adds another fact. The game keeps going until the chain is broken by someone forgetting part of the chain. (The instructor can participate in the chain, as well, to experience the difficulty and fun of remembering.)

Grammar Tip

Conjunctions are words that connect other words, phrases or clauses in a sentence. This song shows the use of the conjunctions "and," "so," "but," "if" and "when" in natural context.

✓ Extension Activities

1. A Japanese haiku is a short poem, usually about Nature or a person's mood. Traditional Haiku poems have three lines and usually five syllables in the first line, seven syllables in the second line and five syllables in the third line. The lines in this haiku are shorter.

   Here is a haiku on the topic of housekeeping by Kobayashi Issa (translated by Robert Haas):

   > Don't worry, spiders
   > I keep house
   >   Casually.

   casually: not carefully

Tell what this poem says in your own words. Why would a spider worry about someone keeping house carefully? What would you say to a spider in *your* house? (You might say "Watch out, spiders. I keep house carefully.")

2. "I Woke Up This Morning" is a song about choices—to clean or cook or fix a roof or play a fiddle. The following poem, by the American poet Maya Angelou, imagines a woman in pre-American Civil War times (before 1861) telling what she has to do on a particular day:

Woman Work
I've got the children to tend
The clothes to mend
The floor to mop
The food to shop
Then the chicken to fry
The baby to dry
I got company to feed
The garden to weed
I've got the shirts to press
The tots to dress
The cane to be cut
I gotta clean up this hut
Then see about the sick
And the cotton to pick.

Shine on me, sunshine
Rain on me, rain
Fall softly, dewdrops
And cool my brow again.

Storm, blow me from here
With your fiercest wind
Let me float across the sky
'Til I can rest again.

Fall gently snowflakes
Cover me with white
Cold icy kisses and
Let me rest tonight.

Sun, rain, curving sky
Mountains, oceans, leaf and stone
Star shine, moon glow
You're all that I can call my own.

Maya Angelou

tend: take care of
cane: sugar cane on plantations of Southern U.S., usually cut by
    African-Americans in pre- and post-Civil War times
hut: small house
cotton to pick: meaning, in the fields of the South

a) Can you picture the scene that Angelou is painting with words? Try to describe (in writing or drawing) the scene of the first fourteen lines. Then describe the scene of the next four stanzas (parts). Describe how the woman feels. Have you ever felt like this?

b) What does the title "Woman Work" mean?

c) Read the poem aloud pausing only at the end of each of the first four-teen lines. Then look carefully at the rest of the lines and mark where pauses should come.

Hints:

• Commas may indicate a pause or change in pitch;

• A pause does not always come at the end of a line of poetry because a line may break in the middle of a clause.

I WOKE UP THIS MORNING

Part 1

Verse 1

1   I woke up this morning
2   And surveyed the room.
3   It was dusty and dirty
4   So I grabbed a broom.
5   I do not like cleaning
6   That's one thing for sure
7   But I can't stand the mess, even more.

Chorus 1

8   I don't like it,
9   You don't like it.
10   Cleaning's never fun,
11   Cleaning's never done,
12   Cleaning's never fun.
13   I don't like it,
14   You don't like it.
15   Cleaning is a bore,
16   Cleaning is a chore,
17   That's for sure.

Part 2

Verse 2

18   I woke up this morning
19   Said, "I'm in the mood—
20   I think I'll start cookin',
21   I'll fix us some food."

22   I do enjoy cooking

23   If I am in charge.

24   I do it my way and I make my
portions large.

Chorus 2

25   I enjoy it,

26   You enjoy it.

27   Cookin's always fun,

28   Even just for one

29   Cookin's always fun.

30   I enjoy it,

31   You enjoy it.

32   Cooking makes me smile.

33   I'm happy for a while

34   When I cook.

Part 3

Verse 3

35   I woke up this morning

36   And surveyed my place.

37   The roof, it was leaking,

38   There was rain on my face.

39   It started to thunder

40   I trembled with fear.

41   Then I called the landlord

42   "Please come over here."

Chorus 3

43   "I can't do it.

44   You must do it.

45   Fixin' roofs is hard

46   Please be on your guard,

47   Fixin' roofs is hard.

48   You're the landlord

49   I'm the tenant.

50   What else can I say?

51   (Sometimes I am glad

52   That I rent.)"

Part 4

Verse 4

53   I woke up this morning

54   The whole place looked fine.

55   It was tidy and cosy

56   For the very first time.

57   I got out my fiddle

58   And started to play.

59   My neighbour's complaining

60   That I've ruined his day.

Chorus 4

61   I'm in trouble

62   Double trouble

63   Have to quiet down,

64   Either that, or just leave town,

65   Have to quiet down.

66   Here's my solution

67　To my noise pollution.

68　"Come up and join the fun,

69　Two's more fun than one

70　That's for sure!"

71　Two's more fun than one

72　That's for sure!

Glossary

Part 1

surveyed: looked around

for sure: certainly, "yes"

can't stand: don't like

mess: a lot of things mixed up, not tidy

chore: work

Part 2

in the mood: feel like doing some particular thing

cookin': cooking, in casual speech

in charge: the "boss"

my way: the way I like to do it

portions: parts or shares of something

Part 3

leaking: water coming through a hole

trembled: shook

landlord: a person who owns a building or land that is rented out to others

fixin': fixing, in casual speech

be on your guard: be careful

tenant: a person paying rent for the temporary use of the land or buildings of another person

Part 4

tidy: neat, orderly, not messy

cosy: nice, giving a warm feeling

fiddle: a violin

double trouble: a lot of trouble

solution: answer

noise pollution: unpleasant sounds,
not peace and quiet

Seasons Come and Go

Theme: Weather in Canada
Pronunciation Focus: Linking / Reduction
Structure: Present Perfect Tense

A student of English was once asked, "What is the most interesting thing about Canada?" He replied, "That's easy—the weather. It's always changing!"

Although a large part of Canada has four seasons, the length of the seasons is different in different parts of the country. In some areas of northern Canada, winter snows last six months, or longer. In Victoria, British Columbia, they say it is always springtime.

Listening to the Song

1. The first time you listen to the song, try to imagine (picture) each season.

2. The second time you listen to the song, do *one* of the following activities.

   a) Jot down the key words you hear so that you can describe the seasons in your own words. Use a chart like this one:

Season	*Words*	*Description*
Summer		
Autumn		
Winter		
Spring		

   b) Fill in the missing words in the following cloze exercise. For this exercise, the missing words are verbs and adjectives.

   ### Seasons Come and Go

   #### Introduction
   1 You have travelled far, and you've travelled wide.
   2 You've _____ oceans, hills, and the countryside.
   3 But have you been to a place I _____
   4 Where each season puts on a _____ show?
   5 Have you ever _____ to a place I know
   6 Where the seasons _____, and the seasons _____?

   #### Verse I
   7 Have you ever been to Canada in summer?
   8 The days are _____, the skies are _____ and clear,
   9 The grass is _____, and flowers dot the landscape.
   10 You'll never want to _____ when summer's here.

   #### Chorus
   11 Seasons _____ and seasons _____,
   12 The weather's always changin'.
   13 Sun or snow? You never _____,
   14 The weather's always _____.

Verse 2

15 Have you ever been to Canada in autumn?

16 The leaves turn _____ and _____ in the trees.

17 The air is _____ and _____ come October.

18 You'll have to _____ here once you _____ that breeze.

(Repeat Chorus)

Verse 3

19 Have you ever been to Canada in winter?

20 The kids are _____ hockey on the ice.

21 I know that winter can be quite _____,

22 But learn to skate, and winter can be nice.

(Repeat Chorus)

Verse 4

23 Have you ever been to Canada in springtime?

24 There's a day in spring when flowers start to _____.

25 Though spring is _____, it's well worth all the waiting.

26 One day in May will _____ all your gloom.

(Repeat Chorus, twice)

✓ Pronunciation Focus

1. When one word ends in a consonant sound, and the next one begins with a vowel, we link (blend) them together when we speak. This helps to keep the rhythm of English. An example is "Don't Give Up" (Song 1).

   What words would you link when you sing the chorus of "Seasons Come and Go"? Practice saying or singing the chorus with special attention to linking.

   If you need more information about linking, see "To the Student" (page xiv).

2. The spoken rhythm of English also requires contractions. For example, the weather's always changing. The verb "to be" often loses a vowel as it joins with the word before it. Auxiliary verbs like "will" and "have" sometimes lose the first consonant and a vowel ("I'll" and "I've.")

   Find the other contractions in the song and say the lines without contracting to see how the rhythm is upset.

Cultural Discussion

1. How does the singer feel about the weather in Canada? Explain your answer. How do the Canadians you have met seem to feel about Canadian weather?

2. Describe to a partner how you feel about the weather where you live now. Do you enjoy the changing seasons in Canada?

3. Did you have to buy new clothes when you came to Canada? If yes, what did you buy? Did you have to buy clothes for the cold weather or for the warm weather?

4. Do you like winter sports like skating or skiing? Winter sports are sometimes expensive hobbies. Are there winter sports that are not expensive?

5. Sometimes people say that the weather in Canada has an effect on the "Canadian personality." Is there such a thing as a national personality? How do such stereotypes get started?

Activities

1. Name the seasons of the place you live now, and write down two words or phrases to describe each one. For example, hot and humid or cold and windy. Then name and describe the seasons in the place where you were born.

    Compare the weather in the two places. Tell in sentences which one is hotter, colder, wetter, nicer, etc.

2. Ask another student the following questions, and add your own questions to the list. If the student answers "yes" to any of the questions, ask the student "where" and "when" he or she did it.

    Have you ever climbed a mountain? (where?, when?)
    Have you ever crossed a sea?
    Have you ever seen a rainbow?
    Have you ever made Chinese tea?
    _____?
    _____?

    Write down the student's answers, and report to the class. For example, "Juan climbed a mountain in Peru in 1989." (Note that in the answer you must use simple past tense instead of present perfect tense because you are giving the date.)

Grammar Tip

"Ever" is a word that means "at any time in the present or past." It is commonly used in questions in the present perfect tense. For example, "Have you ever been to Canada?"

✓ Extension Activities

1. Songs have been written about every season, probably in every language. In English, songs like "Summertime"[1] and "Winter Wonderland"[2] are very famous. The seasons are usually at their best in these songs.

    Here is a Japanese haiku about winter. As we described on page 32, a Japanese haiku is a short poem, usually about Nature or the poet's mood. Haiku poems have three lines and usually five syllables in the first line, seven syllables in the second line and five syllables in the third line.
    a) What is the feeling in this poem, and do you agree with it?

    > Who can stay indoors
    > on such a day with the sun
    > dazzling on new snow!

    Kikaku, translated by Harry Behn

    b) Work with a partner on a sentence of seventeen syllables about the season you are in. Arrange your sentence into three lines. Does it say something in a new way? Is the thought clear? Does it read like a poem?
    Here is one example:

    > I hope spring comes soon;
    > winter is getting me down
    > and I need to smile.

2. Canadian poet Peter van Toorn has written a haiku poem about Nature that makes its effect through exaggeration:

---

[1] "Summertime" from *Porgy and Bess* by George Gershwin, DuBose Heyward, and Ira Gershwin. 1935.
[2] "Winter Wonderland" by Dick Smith and Felix Bernard, 1934. W.B. Music Corporation, renewed.

Mountain Stars
Up in Megantic
the stars are so thick
they stick to the roof of your mouth.
Peter van Toorn

a) Megantic is a small town in northern Quebec where city lights do not interfere with seeing the stars in the night sky. Can you see and *feel* this poem?

b) Van Toorn's playful image can be imitated. Think about a place you have been, or dreamed about. For example,

Over in Bangkok
the flowers are so thick
You hear a "crunch" when you walk.

Is this an exaggeration that helps you to picture Bangkok, a city in Thailand? Try creating your own image:

Up (or over) in_____
the_____are so_____
they_____.

SEASONS COME AND GO

Introduction

1 You have travelled far, and you've travelled wide.

2 You've seen oceans, hills, and the countryside.

3 But have you been to a place I know

4 Where each season puts on a special show?

5 Have you ever been to a place I know

6 Where the seasons come, and the seasons go?

Verse I

7 Have you ever been to Canada in summer?

8 The days are long, the skies are blue and clear,

9 The grass is green, and flowers dot the landscape.

10 You'll never want to leave when summer's here.

Chorus

11 Seasons come and seasons go,

12 The weather's always changin'.

13 Sun or snow? You never know,

14 The weather's always changing.

Verse 2

15 Have you ever been to Canada in autumn?

16 The leaves turn gold and sparkle in the trees.

17 The air is fresh and lively come October.

18 You'll have to stay here once you feel that breeze.

(Repeat Chorus)

Verse 3

19 Have you ever been to Canada in winter?

20 The kids are playing hockey on the ice.

21 I know that winter can be quite depressing,

22 But learn to skate, and winter can be nice.

(Repeat Chorus)

Verse 4

23 Have you ever been to Canada in springtime?

24 There's a day in spring when flowers start to bloom.

25 Though spring is short, it's well worth all the waiting.

26 One day in May will banish all your gloom.

(Repeat Chorus)

Glossary

travel far and wide: do a lot of travelling, to many places

dot: scatter here and there

landscape: a view of land

sparkle: to be bright, glowing

depressing: sad

bloom: open up

well worth all the waiting: a phrase meaning "you'll be glad you were patient"

banish: make something or someone go away

gloom: sadness

Sing Me Your Song

Theme: Sharing Multicultural Celebrations
Pronunciation Focus: Rhythm
Structure: Real Conditional

Holidays and religious holy days are special events for those who celebrate them. When people from many different countries come together to live, they may celebrate holidays and holy days at different times and in different ways.

While everyone in North America shares such holidays as New Year's Day and Labour Day, other days are special for particular groups of people. Canadians observe July 1, Canada Day,

49

as their national holiday. People from the United States observe July 4, Independence Day, as their national holiday. While many Canadians celebrate January 1 as New Year's Day, Vietnamese and Chinese Canadians celebrate another New Year in February. Easter and Christmas have special meaning for Christians. For Jews, Passover, Yom Kippur and Hanukkah are important. Muslims have a special celebration at the end of their month of fasting (Ramadan).

Although it is important to keep our own traditions, sometimes we feel left out when other people celebrate different holidays belonging to their traditions. Once we understand more about the traditions of other people, we can share in their community. This song really says, "Please teach me about your customs and religion so that I can appreciate them too."

"Sing Me Your Song" does not name religions. Instead it names some of the symbols (signs) of religion, for example, candles and bells. The song also describes some of the customs of religions, for instance, the saying of prayers and the lighting of candles.

Listening to the Song

1. The first time you listen, just enjoy the song.

2. The second time you listen to the song, try the following exercise.
   a) Write down the different customs and symbols that are mentioned in the song.
   b) Compare your list with another student's. See if altogether you have six items.
   c) Then try to describe the main idea of the song. Compare your main idea with the main ideas of other students.

Pronunciation Focus

When you sing a song, the melody tells you the rhythm. Saying or chanting a song can also help you learn the rhythms of English speech. Chanting is saying the lines of a song, or a poem, in a highly rhythmic way. "Sing Me Your Song" is a good song to chant.

1. To "warm up," say the following nonsense syllables, stressing the "ta's,"
   but not the "ti's." (Tá ti rhymes with mómmy.)

        Tá ti tá ti tá ti tá

2. Clap when you say ta.

        Tá ti tá ti tá ti tá
        cl   cl   cl   cl

3. Instead of tá ti, say the words to the first verse of the song, clapping to
   the accented syllables:

        If you práy from mórn 'til níght,
        cl   cl   cl   cl

        Sáy one práyer for mé.
        cl   cl   cl

        If you líght eight cándles bríght,
        cl   cl   cl   cl

        Líght one pléase for mé.
         cl   cl   cl

        If you máke the chúrch bells ríng,
        cl   cl   cl   cl

        If you jóin a chóir to síng.
        cl   cl   cl   cl

        Ríng one béll
         cl   cl

        And síng one sóng for mé.
          cl   cl   cl

4. Similarly, add accent marks over the stressed syllables of the second verse,
   and chant that verse as well. Don't forget to clap. You can also stamp your
   feet. Have fun.

5. The ta ti method of practicing rhythm can be used with any song.

✓ Cultural Discussion

Discuss the following questions with other students.

1. In which religions do people pray many times a day?

2. In which religions are candles important? What do candles mean in these religions? In which religion do people light eight candles?

3. In which religions are bells rung? What does the ringing of bells mean?

4. For which religions is singing an important part of their celebrations? What religions chant songs? What is the difference between chanting and singing?

5. Is religion a private, personal thing for you, or is it something you like to talk about? Is it important to understand something about other religions?

6. Does a religious belief help people when they mourn the loss of someone they love? Is mourning easier when people share it?

✓ Activities

1. Match the custom in the song with a religion that practices that custom:

Buddhism	1) pray at least five times a day
Christianity	2) light eight candles during Hanukkah
Judaism	3) ring bells as part of ceremonies
Islam	4) sing songs or chant
Native Peoples' religions	5) meditate

2. Make a list of additional spiritual symbols, beliefs and customs you know about. Then see if other students can give you the name of a group that uses these symbols or beliefs or customs. Examples of beliefs and customs might be reincarnation, respect for parents, union with the natural world.

3. If you feel comfortable doing so, try to translate one of your prayers or religious songs into English. Show your translations to each other. Do you see any similarity between your prayers and religious songs and those of other students? Do different religions pray for the same things?

4. Most of us learn about right and wrong when we are small children. Write down some of the "do's" and "don'ts" you learned as a child. Compare your list with those of other students. For example,

Do's	Don'ts
Obey your parents	Steal

5. Have you ever meditated? If your answer is "yes", try to explain it to someone else who has never meditated.

6. Case Study

    Osman is busy getting ready for a special religious holiday that is traditional in the country where he was born. He talks about it a lot in class. Although Boris does not share Osman's religion, he is very interested and asks many questions about the holiday and about Osman's religion. Osman wonders if he should try to invite Boris to dinner on his holiday.

    Why do you think Boris asks so many questions? Should Osman include Boris? How do you think Osman's family would react if he invited Boris?

7. How about singing a song in another language for your classmates? First translate the title and tell what the song is about.

> **Grammar Tip**
> We can talk about facts or things that are usually true using an "if" sentence. This kind of sentence uses the present tense in both parts or clauses. For example, "If you go to the grocery store, you can buy some milk." We can also use the imperative form in the second clause –"If you pray...Say one prayer for me"– to express a request, command, advice or encouragement. These are examples of the real or possible conditional.

✓ Extension Activities

1. Sharing songs can lead to sharing dreams. "Dream Variation" by the American poet Langston Hughes was published in the 1920s. The dreamer is a black American.

Dream Variation

To fling my arms wide
In some place of the sun,
To whirl and to dance
Till the white day is done.
Then rest at cool evening
Beneath a tall tree
While night comes on gently,
    Dark like me—
That is my dream!

To fling my arms wide
In the face of the sun,
Dance! Whirl! Whirl!
Till the quick day is done.
Rest at pale evening...
A tall, slim tree...
Night coming tenderly
    Black like me.

Langston Hughes

variation: doing the same thing in a different way
fling: throw
whirl: turn very fast
pale: very little colour
slim: thin

a) What is the wish of the dreamer? Why does the dreamer have two similar dreams?

b) This poem has images of light and dark. What things are light? What things are dark? How is each one good?

c) Look at the verbs in the poem. Notice how "fling," "whirl" and "dance" contrast with "rest"? Does contrast mean one is better than the other?

d) What is the feeling or mood of the poem? Does the poet feel free to whirl and dance? Or is he longing to be free to whirl and dance? Remember that the poem was first published in the 1920s, not so long after the American Civil War ended in 1865. If the poet were alive today, would he write the same poem?

2. Finding similarities among religions is a useful effort because sometimes people see only differences between themselves and people who do not have the same background. Concentrating on cultural differences can lead to practises that cause great harm, as described in the following poem by Canadian Jim Wong-Chu. This poem recalls the discrimination against Chinese immigrants who came to Canada in the late 1800s to work on the first railroad across Canada, the Canadian Pacific Railway.

Equal Opportunity
in early canada
when railways were highways

each stop brought new opportunities

there was a rule

    the chinese could only ride
    the last two cars
    of the trains

that is

until a train derailed
killing all those
in front

(the chinese erected an altar and thanked buddha)

a new rule was made

    the chinese must ride
    the front two cars
    of the train

that is

until another accident
claimed everyone
in the back

(the chinese erected an altar and thanked buddha)

after much debate
common sense prevailed

the chinese are now allowed
to sit anywhere
on any train

derailed: went off the rails
erected: built
buddha: the God of Buddhism
claimed: hurt or killed

Tell what the poem is about in your own words, and explain the final three lines. Is the poem humorous? Can serious poems be humorous? What does the poem's title mean?

3. If you have read the poem "Woman Work" (page 33), compare the dream of that poem with the dream of "Dream Variation." What dreams do the two poets share?

SING ME YOUR SONG

Introduction

1 We all come from many nations
2 And we bring our celebrations
3 But we like to share
4 The other ones as well.

Verse 1

5 If you pray from morn 'til night,
6 Say one prayer for me.
7 If you light eight candles bright,
8 Light one please for me.
9 If you make the church bells ring,
10 If you join a choir to sing,
11 Ring one bell
12 And sing one song for me.

Chorus

13 Teach me your prayer.
14 Sing me your song.
15 If you'll share it,
16 I'll sing along.

(Repeat Chorus)

Verse 2

17 And if you choose to meditate,
18 Share your peace with me.
19 If you mourn for someone's fate,
20 Share your woe with me.
21 If you make the church bells ring,

22   If you join a choir to sing,

23   Ring one bell

24   And sing one song for me.

(Repeat Chorus, twice)

Glossary

celebrations: observing special events with ceremonies or festivities

morn: short form of the word "morning"

choir: a group of people who sing together

choose: decide

meditate: think quietly and deeply about something spiritual

peace: quiet, order and security; the opposite of violence

mourn: remember with sadness someone who has died

fate: what happens to a person

woe: sadness

Theme: Money, Values
Pronunciation Focus: Contrastive Stress
Structure: Unreal Conditional

If I Won a Million Dollars

What will $1,000,000 buy? What would you do if you won a million dollars? This is fun to think about, and people can come up with some wild ideas. In this song, "If I Won a Million Dollars," two people have a conversation about what they would do if they suddenly had $1,000,000. The song is meant to be funny but, at the same time, to get people thinking and talking about the value of money in our lives.

Listening to the Song

1. First, just listen for enjoyment.

2. Listen again without looking at the words. Listen for the different view-points of the two people who are singing this song.

3. The third time you listen, pay attention to either the man or the woman, and write down key words, such as nouns and verbs, to help you remember what the singer says.

    Summarize the singer's views. Then compare your list with someone who chose to pay attention to the other singer.

    Which point of view do you agree with? Which point of view "wins" in the song?

✓ Pronunciation Focus

In an English sentence, content words (nouns, main verbs, adverbs, adjectives, question words, and demonstrative pronouns) are stressed, and one word gets more stress than all the other words. Usually this is the last content word in the sentence. For example:

> I didn't *do* it.

We also give added stress to words we want to call attention to.

> *I* didn't do it. *He* did.
> Put the book *in* the bookcase, not *on* it.

Notice how the male singer in the song says the sentence "What would I do with a million dollars?" What word does he stress (say louder and higher)? Why does he over-stress that word? Read the first verse aloud, and work with a partner to predict what words would receive contrastive stress. (Listen for words that are louder and higher.)

If you need more information about stress, please see "To the Student" (page xiv).

Cultural Discussion

1. The two people in this song have different ideas about money. What are some good things that money can't buy (for example, a warm summer day, the laughter of friends)?

2. What do North Americans buy with their money? Make a list. What do people from your original country buy? Compare your lists with those of other students to find similarities.

3. What things have you observed that North Americans value most? Make a list that might include different kinds of things such as family, religion, work, money, peace, etc. What do you value most? Compare your lists with those of other students. Are there any values that *everyone* shares?

4. Which is more important: to save money for a "rainy day" or to spend it and enjoy life *today*? Discuss your opinion with a group of students and try to convince them of your point of view.

Activities

1. Look again at the song, "If I Won a Million Dollars," to see what singers A and B want to do with $1,000,000. List the things, if any, that you might do if you won $1,000,000. Then write a sentence or paragraph about what you would do if you won $1,000,000.

2. Turn the song, "If I Won a Million Dollars," into a skit (a short play). Pretend you are Singer A and your partner is Singer B. Singer A should try to convince Singer B to spend the $1,000,000. Singer B should try to convince Singer A to give it away. You can use the following phrases:

   why don't you...
   perhaps you could...
   don't you think...

3. Interview another student, asking how winning a million dollars would complicate his or her life. What would change if he or she won a million dollars? Report the answer to the class.

Grammar Tip
"If I Won a Million Dollars" is an "unreal" conditional structure. It expresses a hypothetical (imaginary) condition and its probable result. The simple past tense is in the "if" clause and "would" plus infinitive in the following clause.

✓ **Extension Activities**

1. Singer B in "If I Won a Million Dollars" says the best things in life are free. Here are lines from a poem by Duke Redbird, a First Nation writer and broadcaster, about what is most valuable to him.

    > Oh give me the rain and the wind,
    > And the mist of a summer draped lake,
    > Give me the warm arms of a morning dawn
    > And the tender kiss of a summer breeze,
    > Shaking the sunlight from the poplar leaves.
    > And give me the caress of a woman's hand
    > Soft as a moment, alive as the land ....
    >
    > *Duke Redbird, "Alive as the Land"*

    draped: covered
    poplar: a tree
    caress: touching with love

    a) How is nature described in these lines from Duke Redbird's poem? What comparisons are made? What attitude toward nature does this comparison reveal? What is the attitude towards people?
    b) With a partner, decide what you think Singer A and Duke Redbird might say to each other about money if they were to meet? What would Singer B say to Duke Redbird?
    c) How does this list of wishes compare to Maya Angelou's list in her poem "Woman Work" (page 33)?

2. Sometimes we come to value something only after we lose it. What does this poem by Leonard Cohen value?

    > **For Anne**
    > With Annie gone,
    > Whose eyes to compare
    > With the morning sun?
    >
    > Not that I did compare
    > But I do compare
    > Now that she's gone.
    >
    > *Leonard Cohen*

a) Where is Annie? Why do you think she left?

b) What is the mood of the poem? How would you describe the poet's feelings?

c) Does the writer miss Annie? How do you know?

IF I WON
A MILLION DOLLARS

Singer A. Excuse me, would you like to buy a lottery ticket? You could win a million dollars!

Singer B. Um, I don't think so. What would I do with a million dollars?

Verse I (Singer B)

1   If I won a million dollars,
2   I would give it all away.
3   I don't need a million dollars
4   It's not worth a summer's day.
5   I don't need a million dollars
6   It would complicate my life.
7   I'd need some help to spend it
8   I might have to find a wife.

Chorus I (Singer B)

9   Hi ho, oh no
10 Money will get you in trouble.
11 Hi ho, oh no
12 Money will get you in trouble.

Singer A. Man, I know what I'd do with it!

Verse 2 (Singer A)

13 If I won a million dollars,
14 I would buy a fancy car.
15 Then I'd buy a great big house

16   And live like a movie star.

17   I'd share that house with my friends

18   And have parties by the sea.

19   I'd even ask my relatives

20   To share my wealth with me.

Chorus 2 (Singer A)

21   Money, I want more

22   I'd rather be rich than poor.

23   Money, I need more

24   I'd rather be rich than poor.

**Singer B. Well, I'm impressed.
Money doesn't scare you!**

Verse 3 (Singer B)

25   If I won a million dollars,

26   I would give it all to you.

27   You're not afraid of being rich

28   You know just what to do.

29   I still believe with all my heart

30   The best things in life are free.

31   But I'm listening to your point of view

32   And your plan sounds good to me.

Chorus 1

33   Hi ho, oh no

34   Money will get you in trouble.

35   Hi ho, oh no

36   Money will get you in trouble.

Singer A. I think I see where you're coming from!

Verse 4 (Singer A)

37　I know that money's funny
38　And can mess you up for sure.
39　But one thing is for certain
40　Without it you'll be poor.
41　If you give me your money,
42　I'll make sure you have some fun
43　Relaxing with my relatives
44　At my cottage in the sun.

Chorus 2

45　Money, I want more
46　I'd rather be rich than poor.
47　Money, I need more
48　I'd rather be rich than poor.

Glossary
worth: value
complicate: make difficult
hi ho: meaningless expression,
  for rhythm and effect
wealth: money, riches
the best things in life are free:
  a famous saying
your point of view: what you think
sounds: seems
coming from: what you mean
funny: strange, unpredictable
mess you up: make you do unwise
  things
for certain: for sure

It's Hard to be Polite in English

Theme: Greetings and Small Talk
Pronunciation Focus: Intonation
Structure: Real Conditional

In North America when people meet informally, they greet each other politely. They say "hello" or "hi" and sometimes ask a question that is confusing because it does not require an answer.

How many times have you been asked "How are you?" by people who don't stop for an answer? What does that phrase mean in English?

This is a song about polite questions that confuse ESL students.

Listening to the Song

1. First, just listen to the song for enjoyment.

2. The second time you listen, write down the questions and greetings that confuse the singer.

Pronunciation Focus

1. Because English intonation (the pattern of pitch highs and lows) has more variety than some languages, students sometimes find intonation difficult to hear and to imitate. Listen to your teacher saying these phrases of greeting and response with English intonation. Imitate that intonation.

> Hi, how are you?
> Very well, thank you.
> So-So.
> Not bad.
> You're looking well.
>
> Hi there, what's new?
> Oh, not much.
> Well…

For more information on intonation, please see "To the Student" (page xiv).

Cultural Discussion

1. What are the main topics of conversation when people meet accidentally on the street in the place where you live now? Are these topics the same as in the place where you grew up? Explain the differences.

2. How long would such a conversation last in each place (where you live now and where you lived before you came to Canada)? For example, a student from Egypt says thirty minutes; an English teacher says thirty seconds.

3. What polite phrases confuse you? Do the words mean what they *seem* to mean (for example, "You must stop by for tea.")?

4. What customs in North America puzzle you? What customs in your country would puzzle a visitor from North America?

Activities

1. With a partner, decide what answers you will give when someone asks the questions in the song. Check your answers with other students' answers. Tell what each phrase in the song really means, in other words.

2. Decide in groups what these phrases mean:

    "Let's do lunch."
    "You must come over to my place sometime."
    "Catch ya later."
    "See you around."
    "Hang in there."
    "Get outta here."

    Make up a dialogue with one of these phrases.

Grammar Tip

Real or possible conditional sentences can express a command or a request, as in "If you pray ... Say one prayer for me" (see Song 7 "Sing Me Your Song"). The "if" clause can also be followed by questions, as in the song, "It's Hard to be Polite in English": "If you say ..., *do you really want the truth?"* and "If a friend says ..., *should I say,* "You look great too?"* The present tense is used in both clauses.

✓ Extension Activity

1. Communication (the sending and receiving of messages) often breaks down, even among people who speak the same language. However, the following Inuit poem tells of a time long ago when people and animals talked to and understood each other, and if you said you wanted something to happen, it happened.

    ### Magic Words
    In the very earliest time,
    when both people and animals lived on earth,
    a person could become an animal if he wanted to
    and an animal could become a human being.
    Sometimes they were people
    and sometimes animals
    and there was no difference.

All spoke the same language.
That was the time when words were like magic.
The human mind had mysterious powers.
A word spoken by chance
might have strange consequences.
It would suddenly come alive
and what people wanted to happen could happen—
Nobody could explain this:
That's just the way it was.

Anonymous poem, after [in the manner of] Nalungiaq,
translated by Edward Field

by chance: accidentally, unexpectedly

consequences: results

That's the way it was: an expression meaning that we can't explain why it
    happened

a) What is the relationship between people and animals in this poem?
How is it different from the relationship between people and animals in
our world?
b) Do you wish you lived in the time that this Inuit poem talks about?
What would you say if your words were magic?

It's Hard to be Polite in English

Verse 1

1 If you say, "Hi, how are you?"
2 Do you really want the truth?
3 Should I say how bad my back hurts
4 And show you my aching tooth?
5 Or should I say, "Very well,
   thank you"
6 And tell an enormous lie?
7 It's hard to be polite in English
8 I must smile when I want to cry.

Chorus

9   It's so hard to be polite
10 When the language you're using
   is new.
11 It's so easy to make a mistake.
12 Oh, what's a poor student to do?
13 What's a poor student to do?
   Oh yeah.

Verse 2

14 If a friend says, "You're looking
   great!"
15 Should I say, "You look great too?"
16 Are we just being polite
17 Or is what we're saying true?

(Repeat Chorus)

Verse 3

18   I'm not sure how I should respond

19   When a friend says, "Hi there,
       what's new?"

20   How much does he want to know?

21   Tell me the right thing to do!

(Repeat Chorus twice)

Glossary

enormous: very large

great: very well

respond: answer

I Dreamt I Was a Child Again

Theme: Immigration, Travel, Families
Pronunciation Focus: Rhythm and Intonation
Structure: Subjunctive

When you were a child, did you ever dream about travelling to faraway places? What did you imagine such places would be like? Did any of your dreams come true? Have your dreams changed as you have grown older?

73

Listening to the Song

1. Listen to the song first for enjoyment.

2. Then listen to find out:
   a) what the mother sang to the child about,
   b) what the mother sang to the sixteen-year-old about, and
   c) what the singer sings to her child about.

3. Listen again to hear if the singer's dream came true, and whether she is happy now.

✓ Pronunciation Focus

1. In order to sing the lines of this song smoothly and rhythmically, we link words, for example:

   I dreamt I was a child again

   Listen to the chorus again (lines 9-12) and circle the linked (blended) words.

   ### Chorus
   I wish I were a child again.
   There are dreams only children can know.
   I wish I were a child again
   Dreaming dreams of the places I'd go.

   For a discussion of linking, please see "To the Student" (page xiv).

Cultural Discussion

1. What is the mother like in this song? Does she remind you of anyone you know?

2. Do you want your children to see faraway places? Why or why not? What are the pros and cons of children leaving home?

3. Do all parents you know sing songs to their children? If yes, what are the songs about? If no, what other rituals do you remember from when you were a child (for example, taking walks, telling stories, teaching games, teaching what's right and what's wrong)?

4. What do night-time dreams mean? Do people from different countries have different answers for this question?

Activities

1. Tell a partner about a dream you have had that made you happy. (If you can't remember one, make one up.)

2. Imagine what the mother in this song wrote in a letter after the singer crossed the sea; then write that letter.

3. Write an essay describing your dreams (day or night) as a child and how they have changed as you have grown older.

Grammar Tip

This song says "I dreamt I *was* a child again" and "I wish I *were* a child again." Why the difference in the form of the verb "to be"? "I was" follows the verb "dream," an ordinary verb that takes the simple past in both clauses. But "wish" is a special verb that takes the past subjunctive "were" in the second clause. To "wish" is to desire something that is unreal. For example, "I wish I had a million dollars."

✓ Extension Activities

1. The following song lyrics by Bob Merrill are about someone from a very small town (Mira) who has moved to a big city and is feeling quite lost. Can you understand this person's feelings?

> **Mira (Can You Imagine That?)**
> I came on two buses and a train.
> CAN YOU IMAGINE THAT?
> CAN YOU IMAGINE THAT?
> Two buses and a train.
>
> Would you believe, would you believe
> This is the first I've travelled.
> I come from a town, the kind of town
> where you live in a house 'til the house falls down,
> but if it stands up, you stay there.
> It's funny but that's the way there.

I came from the town of Mira
beyond the bridges of Saint Claire.
I guess you've never heard of Mira,
It's very small but still it's there.
They have the very greenest trees
and skies as bright as flame.
But what I liked the best in Mira
is everybody knew my name.

CAN YOU IMAGINE THAT?
CAN YOU IMAGINE THAT?
Ev'rybody knew my name.

A room that is strange is never cozy,
A place that is strange is never sweet.
I want to have a chair that knows me,
and walk a street that knows my feet.
I'm very far from Mira now,
and there's no turning back.
I have to find a place,
I've got to find a place
where ev'rything can be the same.
A street that I can know,
and places I can go
where everybody knows my name.

CAN YOU IMAGINE THAT?
CAN YOU IMAGINE THAT?
Ev'rybody knew my name.

Bob Merrill

Mira and Saint Claire: small towns
cozy: warm and comfortable
ev'rybody: everybody
ev'rything: everything

2.   a) This song has many idiomatic phrases and expressions. Work with a
partner and decide what you think the following expressions mean:

"Can you imagine?"

"Would you believe?"

"'til the house falls down"

"that's the way"

"everybody knew my name"

"a chair that knows me"

"a street that knows my feet"

b) The lyrics of this song contain many images—the town of Mira, an old house, a strange (new) room, a new street, a new chair, a new town. Some are old and some are new. Which ones are better, in the eyes of the poem?

c) Why is it important that everyone knows the singer's name?

d) Homework: Write a verse or an essay beginning "I come from the town of _____," about your own feelings of moving to a new place.

I Dreamt I Was a Child Again

Verse 1

1   I dreamt I was a child again
2   Feeling happy and silly and free.
3   I asked my mother to sing me
    a song,
4   She sat me down on her knee.
5   She took my hand and sang me a
    song
6   About places far over the sea.
7   I sat there and pictured myself
8   And imagined how happy I'd be.

Chorus

9   I wish I were a child again.
10   There are dreams only children can
    know.
11   I wish I were a child again
12   Dreaming dreams of the places
    I'd go.

Verse 2

13   I dreamt I was sixteen again
14   Feeling restless and wanting to roam.
15   I asked my mother to sing me a
    song
16   About places far from my home.
17   She smiled at me and sang me a
    song

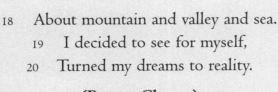

18 About mountain and valley and sea.

19 I decided to see for myself,

20 Turned my dreams to reality.

(Repeat Chorus)

Verse 3

21 And now I'm home with my family

22 Many years after crossing the sea.

23 My daughter asks me to sing her a song,

24 I sit her down on my knee.

25 I take her hand and sing her a song

26 That tells her, "There's no place like home."

27 I'll be darned if I'll give her the notion,

28 I'd be lost if she travelled the ocean.

(Repeat Chorus)

New Chorus

29 I wish I were a child again

30 For I miss that land over the sea.

31 I wish I were a child again

32 Dreaming dreams at my mother's knee.

33 Dreaming dreams at my mother's knee.

34 Dreaming dreams at my mother's knee.

35 Dreaming, dreaming, dreaming...

Glossary

silly: not serious or sensible
pictured: imagined
know: here it means "have"
restless: wanting to get up and go
turned my dreams to reality: did the things I dreamed of doing
"There's no place like home": a famous saying
notion: idea
I'd be lost: I would feel terrible

Musical Notations for Songs

Song 1

Don't Give Up

Song 2

What Are You Gonna Do Today?

Verse 2

I'll do some grocery shopping
(The fridge at home is bare).
And then I'll go and buy some clothes;
I haven't a thing to wear.

Verse 3

Tonight I may go dancing
Or see a movie instead.
Then I might watch television
Before I go to bed.

Song 3

What Do You Do When You Feel Ill?

Verses

Rap   (Spoken)

What do you do   when you feel   ill?   Drink mint tea?   Take a pill?

Go to bed   for   twenty-four hours? Or   wait   for   friends to bring you   flo - wers?

Chorus

Am

Some peo - ple say   "I'm hurt."   Others   hide   their   pain.

Am   G   F   C/E

Some go a lit-tle crazy. _____   Oth-ers act quite sane.   Some get well fast.

F   C/E   F   G   C

Some get well slow.   How do you act when you're sick?   Does it   show?

Verse 2

When I get sick, I go to bed,
Close my eyes and prop my head.
I take a nap for an hour or two.
Soon I'm back to work, feeling good as new.
(What do you do?)

Verse 3

When I get sick, I hate the world.
My hair is straight, but it gets all curled.
I feel like heck, and I look no better.
I get hot, then cold, but can't find a sweater.

Song 4

Good-bye

Verse 2
Good-bye, my friend, adios.
I am sad but it won't show.
We've had our share of good times,
And now it's time to go.

Verse 3
Good-bye, my friend, sayonara.
These are my wishes for you:
May your future be bright,
And your troubles be few.

Song 5

I Woke Up This Morning

Chorus 2 [B]

I en-joy it, You en-joy it. Cook-in's al-ways fun, Ev-en just for one Cook-in's al-ways fun.

I en-joy it, You en-joy it. Cook-ing makes me smile. I'm happy for a while When I cook.

Verse 3

I woke up this morning
And surveyed my place.
The roof, it was leaking,
There was rain on my face.
It started to thunder
I trembled with fear.
Then I called the landlord
'Please come over here.'

Chorus 3

'I can't do it.
You must do it.
Fixin' roofs is hard
Please be on your guard,
Fixin' roofs is hard.
You're the landlord
I'm the tenant.
What else can I say?
(Sometimes I am glad
That I rent.'

Verse 4

I woke up this morning
The whole place looked fine.
It was tidy and cosy
For the very first time.
I got out my fiddle
And started to play.
My neighbour's complaining
That I've ruined his day.

Chorus 4

I'm in trouble
Double trouble
Have to quiet down,
Either that, or just leave town,
Have to quiet down.
Here's my solution
To my noise pollution.
'Come up and join the fun,
Two's more fun than one
That's for sure!'

Song 6

Seasons Come and Go

Verse 2
Have you ever been to Canada in autumn?
The leaves turn gold and sparkle in the trees.
The air is fresh and lively come October.
You'll have to stay here once you feel that breeze.

Verse 3
Have you ever been to Canada in winter?
The kids are playing hockey on the ice.
I know that winter can be quite depressing.
But learn to skate, and winter can be nice.

Verse 4
Have you ever been to Canada in springtime?
There's a day in spring when flowers start to bloom.
Though spring is short, it's well worth all the waiting.
One day in May will banish all your gloom.

Song 7

Sing Me Your Song

Verse 2

And if you choose to meditate,
Share your peace with me.
If you mourn for someone's fate,
Share your woe with me.

If you make the church bells ring,
If you join a choir to sing,
Ring one bell
And sing one song for me.

Song 8

If I Won a Million Dollars

Verses

If I won a mil - lion dol - lars, I would give it all a - way. __

I don't need a mil - lion dol - lars It's not worth a sum - mer's day. __

I don't need a mil - lion dol-lars It would com - pli - cate my life. __

I'd need some help to spend __ it I might have to find __ a wife. __ Hi

Chorus 1

ho, __ oh no __ Mon-ey _ will get you in trou-ble. . Hi

ho, __ oh no __ Mon-ey _ will get you in trou-ble. __

Chorus 2

Mon-ey, ___   I want more   I'd ra-ther be rich ___ than poor.

Mon-ey, ___   I need more   I'd ra-ther be rich ___ than poor.

(Alternate Chorus 1 and Chorus 2)

Verse 2

If I won a million dollars,
I would buy a fancy car.
Then I'd buy a great big house
And live like a movie star.
I'd share that house with my friends
And have parties by the sea.
I'd even ask my relatives
To share my wealth with me.

Verse 3

If I won a million dollars,
I would give it all to you.
You're not afraid of being rich
You know just what to do.
I still believe with all my heart
The best things in life are free.
But I'm listening to your point of view
And your plan sounds good to me.

Verse 4

I know that money's funny
And can mess you up for sure.
But one thing is for certain
Without it you'll be poor.
If you give me your money,
I'll make sure you have some fun
Relaxing with my relatives
At my cottage in the sun.

Song 9

It's Hard to be Polite in English

Verse 3
I'm not sure
How I should respond
When a friend says 'Hi there, what's new?'
How much does he want to know?
Tell me the right thing to do!

Song 10

I Dreamt I Was a Child Again

Verse 2
I dreamt I was sixteen again
Feeling restless and wanting to roam.
I asked my mother to sing me a song,
About places far from my home.
She smiled at me and sang me a song
About mountain and valley and sea.
I decided to see for myself,
Turned my dreams to reality.
(Chorus)

Verse 3
And now I'm home with my family
Many years after crossing the sea.
My daughter asks me to sing her a song,
I sit her down on my knee.
I take her hand and sing her a song
That tells her, 'There's no place like home.'
I'll be darned if I'll give her the notion,
I'd be lost if she travelled the ocean.
(Chorus)

Chorus 2
I wish I were a child again
For I miss that land over the sea.
I wish I were a child again
Dreaming dreams at my mother's knee.

Answer Key

Answers for selected activities (those with a checkmark (✓) beside them in the book) are provided below.

Song 1
Pronunciation Focus (page 2)
1. line I: when I
   line 2: stayed in
   line 3: cold and
   line 6: class is
2. you're = you are
   there's = there is
   life's = life is

Extension Activities (page 4)
2. Hope is inside of us, like a bird that never stops singing. (The poem goes on to say that hope is always there and asks nothing of us.)
3. The lines from the poem by Natasha show that loneliness hurts people just as much as sickness does. The poem imagines something inside of us crying about a different kind of hunger, a hunger for another person to care about us.

Song 2
Pronunciation Focus (page 10)
2. "wheredja" - where did you (go)?
   "whydja" - why did you (come to school late)?

Extension Activities (page 12)
2. Challenge: I know a young *ESL student*
   Who's wise and clever and prudent.

Song 3
Extension Activities (page 19)
2. The best gift is love. The word "only" before "heaven" makes heaven less valuable than love. Joy comes in small amounts like crumbs and leftover bones. Love is the one gift that is not made to seem small. The luckiest people get love.

Song 4
Extension Activities (page 25)
2. a) One possible meaning for this couplet by Wang Bo is that true friends are never really apart even though distance may separate them.

Song 5
Pronunciation Focus (page 31)
2. cleaning, leaking, complaining may be reduced to cleanin', leakin', complainin'

Extension Activities (pages 32-34)
1. The speaker in this haiku poem tells the spider not to worry because the speaker is not careful about keeping the house neat and clean, and so the spider will not be disturbed or killed. A careful housekeeper would not tolerate a spider.
2. a) In the first fourteen lines, the woman in the poem by Maya Angelou is feeling overwhelmed by all the things she is responsible for. The rest of the poem describes how she turns to nature—sun, rain, wind, snow, and moon—for comfort. They are all that she has in the world.
   b) "Women's work" is a phrase once used to mean that certain jobs around the house belonged only to women, for example, mending clothes. Women objected to this and now the phrase is usually used sarcastically, making fun of this idea. The title "Woman Work" sounds like a command: woman, work.

Song 6
Pronunciation Focus (page 42)
1. Linking: come and, weather's always, sun or
2. Contractions: you've, You'll, summer's, weather's, there's, it's

Extension Activities (page 44)
1. a) This haiku sounds like a spontaneous expression of joy at the beauty of the sun shining on fresh snow. Who would want to stay inside and miss this experience?

Song 7

Cultural Discussion (page 52)

Note: Students will add and share details about the meanings of these symbols and ceremonies in their discussions.

1. Many religions encourage prayer one or more times a day. Muslims pray five times a day.
2. Candles are important in many religions. In Judaism, a new candle is lit each day for 8 days during Hanukkah, the festival of lights.
3. Buddhists and Christians ring bells during religious ceremonies.
4. Christians have choirs. Jewish cantors lead songs. Buddhists chant songs. Native peoples chant during special ceremonies.

Activities (page 52)

1. Buddhism 3, 4, 5
   Christianity 3, 4, 5
   Judaism 2, 4
   Islam 1
   Native people's religions 4, 5

Extension Activities (pages 53-56)

1. a) The dreamer wants to dance freely all day and rest at evening. The second dream is almost the same. This wish must be important to the dreamer.

   b) Light: the sun, daylight (white day)
   Dark: gentle night, tender night, me
   In-between: cool, pale evening

   c) In the poem all the images are good: light, dark; white, black; dance, rest. Contrast does not mean any one is better than the other.

   d) The poem gives a feeling of someone who is being held back, someone who is frustrated.

2. A possible summary of "Equal Opportunity": When the railways were first built in Canada (in the latter part of the nineteenth century), Chinese passengers had to ride at the back of the train until an accident occurred which killed the people in front. The Chinese were then told to ride in the front until an accident killed those at the back. After that, they could sit anywhere—not because it was fair, the poem says, but because people were afraid of what would happen if they continued to discriminate.

   The poem is satirical, using humour to say that people will only change if their bad behaviour is proven to hurt *them*.

   "Equal Opportunity" is a term that in recent history has meant a guarantee of opportunities for minority groups. The poet is being ironic (saying the opposite of what you mean) because in this poem "equal opportunity" means an equal chance to be killed in a trainwreck.

Song 8

Pronunciation Focus (page 60)

1. One possible way to give contrastive stress within this song would be as follows:
   If **I** won a million dollars
   I would give it all away.
   I don't **need** a million dollars
   It's **not** worth a summer's day.

Extension Activities (pages 62-63)

1. a) Comparisons that are made in this poem:
   • dawn and the warm arms of a human being
   • a breeze and a kiss
   • a woman's soft hand and a moment
   • the land and a woman's soft hand

   These comparisons have the effect of blurring (making unclear) the distinction between humans and nature.

   c) Maya Angelou's list of wishes is similar to Duke Redbird's. They both see nature as benevolent (kind). However, Maya Angelou sees nature as separate from herself, as something to possess; Duke Redbird sees people and nature as one.

2. a) Annie had left him, perhaps because he did not appreciate her.

   b) The mood is one of loss and regret.

   c) We know the writer misses her because the lines "Whose eyes to compare/With the morning sun?" show that he remembers her beauty and has no one who can take her place.

Song 9

Extension Activities (page 70)

1. a) In the anonymous Inuit poem, the relationship seems to be that people and animals were once interchangeable, that is, one could become the other, and there was no real difference between them.

Song 10

Pronunciation Focus (page 74)

1. I wish I were a child again
    There are dreams only children can know.

I wish I were a child again
Dreaming dreams of the places I'd go.

Extension Activity (page 77)

2. b) The poem suggests that the old things are better because the writer feels a longing for familiar, comfortable things from his small home town of Mira.

c) When everyone knew the person's name, he had an identity. In a new town the singer feels like a nobody. There is no connection between the newcomer and the new place. (This person would understand the poem "Loneliness" in the Extension Activities of Song I.)